Praises for "iDentity"

Many Korean-American young people today are grappling with the profound tensions of an "in-between" generation. They are a step removed from the immigration experience of their elders, yet they are not yet fully assimilated to the culture of their thoroughly "American" peers. This much-needed curriculum can nurture a generation that is uniquely prepared to hear the call to that "in-between-ness" to which the Gospel calls all of us: to be "in," but not "of," the world. There is a marvelous potential here for equipping gifted young people to become the leaders that the church at large desperately needs!
–Dr. Richard J. Mouw, President, Fuller Theological Seminary

Thanks be to God: the resource that we've been waiting for has finally arrived! In this extraordinarily creative curriculum for Korean American youth, as well as their parents, pastors, and teachers, the authors put forth the lessons that must be explored, learned, and practiced. Users will find this curriculum to be a matchless resource for addressing the issues of identity as they relate to culture, Christ, competence, and community in the Korean American context, while also helping our young people develop a robust Christian faith. I enthusiastically commend this resource to the Korean American Christian community.
– Rev. Jeremiah Jungchan Park, Resident Bishop of New York Annual Conference, The United Methodist Church

A very creative, resourceful, well-conceived curriculum based on insightful contextual analysis and faithful biblical exegesis! It powerfully engages complex intercultural experiences of the youth with the message of the Scripture with clarity and openness. The curriculum is a rare accomplishment in the field of the Asian American Christian youth education and multicultural studies. I enthusiastically recommended this work for churches that minister to Korean American youth who struggle with various psycho-social and spiritual issues.
– Dr. Inn Sook Lee, Adjunct Professor of Christian Education, Princeton Theological Seminary

The "iDentity" curriculum is a remarkable gift for the nurture of Korean American youth in the Christian faith. Organized around the four intersecting themes of culture, Christ, competence, and community, the curriculum invites Korean American adolescents into deep dialogue with adults about what it means to embrace a bi-cultural Christian identity in which love of self, God, neighbor, and the earth can flourish. Using Korean American life stories, social science research, media resources, and Biblical stories, the "iDentity" curriculum honestly probes the realities that impede the development of a positive bi-cultural Christian identity, such as systemic racism, as well as the realities that support such identity, such

as the discovery of God-given gifts and passions. The curriculum's content and dialogical methodology are exactly what is needed to enable Korean American youth to candidly probe their own experiences in cultural context and in light of the Biblical witness. In the power of the Holy Spirit, "iDentity" provides a wonderful resource for God's people to navigate the tension between the simple handing over of the Christian faith, and its renewal as younger generations of Korean American Christian receive, probe, and learn to live that faith with courage and commitment in their time and place.
–Dr. Renee House, the Dean of the Seminary, New Brunswick Theological Seminary.

This is a much needed and thoughtful curriculum for Korean-American youths today who are looking for guidance in their struggles regarding identity, self-esteem, personal faith, familial obligation, service for the community, and world issues. Each lesson in the curriculum demonstrates an in-depth understanding of the challenges that the youth living in a bicultural society face, and sheds light on how churches can help them in navigating an increasingly complicated and morally ambiguous world. In addressing the challenges, the curriculum draws upon ancient truths and wisdoms in the Bible and shares their meanings in a fresh way.
–Kwang S. Kim, President, Korean Community Services of Metropolitan New York, Inc.

Despite the fact that Korean immigration history has surpassed the 100 year mark, no church youth curriculum that dealt extensively with the real life crisis caused by clashing identities, cultures, and languages was available for the Korean Americans in North America until now. With the news of the publication of "iDentity," my prayers of petition turned into prayers of gratitude for this tool and the opportunity to impact our future generations. As a fellow Christian educator and Korean immigrant, I am blessedly assured that this curriculum will stir up our second generation Korean Americans because the footsteps of our Korean pioneers have been imprinted in "iDentity." I truly hope and pray that this curriculum's contagious influence on our upcoming generation will nurture the Korean Diaspora to lead as God's vessels to the ends of the earth.
–Rev. Sang Kwon, Education Pastor of Young Nak Presbyterian Church, LA.

A Curriculum for Korean American Christian Youth

Hak Joon Lee, Kevin Park, Kil Jae Park

Christian Education Center

"The title iDenti터 is created by taking the English word "identity" and substituting the Korean letters "터" for its final syllable "-ty," which has the same sound. At the same time, the Korean letter "터" looks similar to the Hebrew word "El", which is a transliteration into English of the Hebrew word(אֵל) meaning "God." The significance of the title "iDenti터" is in its description of Korean American identity as a hybrid of American and Korean with God as its foundation."

Published 2011 by
G2G Christian Education Center
P.O. Box 580303 Flushing, NY 11358-0303
info@g2gcenter.org, 646)220-3258
www.g2gcenter.org

ISBN: 978-1-257-01665-5

Cover designed by Kyuseop Lee (idsketchbook@gmail.com)
Book designed by Sojin Ouh (souh@risd.edu)

G2G Christian Education Center

G2G Christian Education Center is a nonprofit Christian organization, founded in 2007 to address the spiritual, cultural, and social concerns in the Asian American Community.

To

korean american parents

whose sacrifice and love for their children are truly inspirational and one of a kind,

youth pastors and teachers

who untiringly journey together with our teenagers through their dark valleys and to their mountaintops, and

korean american teenagers

whose potentials are truly unlimited in God.

Contents

Foreword

All adolescents seek to establish an identity of their own and spend countless hours of time, energy, and effort in their exploration of one. Identity formation is a complex process for anyone, but it is one that becomes especially complicated when one simultaneously saddles multiple cultures. This is where the challenge and dilemma lie for many Korean American youth when it comes to the task of identity formation. As the nomenclature suggests, Korean American youth are those who live in two different cultural worlds that are often at odds with each other– the world of egalitarian and individualistic Western American culture of the dominant society and the world of hierarchical and collective Korean/Confucian culture found in their homes and ethnic churches.

As such, the struggle for many Korean American youth has been figuring out how to negotiate different cultural demands and expectations that are placed on them by these two competing cultures while trying to remain loyal to both. Unfortunately, the result for many Korean American youth has been the continual oscillation between two cultures without much formal direction or guidance from neither the larger society nor their parents and church leaders. It is no mystery then that studies and research confirm Korean American youth to be at risk for low self-esteem, diffused self-identity, and tumultuous cultural tensions in their families and churches.

In light of such socio-cultural realities of Korean American youth, iDENTITY is a timely and fitting innovation for Korean American youth and their communities who now have a structured guide to help scaffold their multi-faceted experiences. Creatively interweaving the four primary sources of identity formation (culture, Christ, competence, and community), the curriculum is carefully designed as a step-by-step guide for Korean American youth in their journey toward self-discovery through the labyrinth of conflicting cultural values and confusing social expectations and demands.

The curriculum demonstrates excellence in pedagogy, utilizing internet media resources and social scientific data, along with biblical exegetical information. In particular, its dialogical and narrative approach is extremely relevant for contemporary youth who often feel alienated from the traditional indoctrinating form of Christian education. The case examples in the curriculum are relatable and engaging, and they are intended to facilitate introspection and reflection toward one's own struggles and challenges.

iDENTITY indeed is a welcome gift to Korean American churches, educators, parents, and youth alike.

Dr. Josephine M. Kim
Lecturer on Education
Harvard University
Graduate School of Education

Acknowledgements

Crafting a curriculum of this nature is an intergenerational bridge-building work. It has to do with handing down the wisdom and experience ("tradition") of one generation to the next. Much is at stake in the process: not only the historical continuity of the legacy of a community but also its renewed vitality and growth in the future. It would be a mistake, therefore, to dismiss the curriculum as indoctrination by the older generation; rather it should be understood as the renewal of a covenant in which the younger generation freely participates in the communal labor of appropriating the tradition in its own social and cultural contexts. The Scripture is deeply attentive to the significance of this task as the Book of Deuteronomy (6:4-9) captures it in the most telling and eloquent form through the sermons and commitments of Moses and Israelites.

This task of handing down faith experience is an urgent but very complicated matter in the Korean American community because of the profound cultural and social gaps that exist between the first and the second generation Korean Americans. The difference is more than generational; it is rather more like a clash between two very different moral universes—the East and the West.

As the first fruit of G2G Christian Education Center, this curriculum aims to ease the tensions arising from such differences. It is offered to build a bridge that connects the faith, dedication, and aspiration of the parents' generation Korean Americans to the passion, love, creativity of the children's generation.

Bridge building is a collaborative work. There are so many people who participated in and contributed to this bridge building work at its various stages with their prayer, intellectual inputs, and financial and institutional supports. It is my regret that due to space limitations I am not able to thank everyone here for their precious contributions. However, I want to acknowledge at least some of them. I am deeply indebted to the Doorae Community Movement of North America, First United Methodist Church in Flushing (Rev. Joong Urn Kim), Joy Christian Fellowship Church (Rev. Danny Han), Hanaim Church (Rev. Hak Kwon Lee), Seodaejon Central Church (Rev. Rakwon Lee), Mr. Chan Myung Park, Ms. Jee Young Kim for their generous financial, institutional, and moral supports. I also want to thank Dr. Jung Sook Jung, Ms. Hai Young Chun, Rev. Elizabeth Vaneekhoven, and Rev. Joo Whang for their constructive comments on the curriculum, Rev. Joanne Noel and my dear friend Rev. E. J. Emerson for their careful proofreading of the drafts at various stages, and Mr. Kyu Sup Lee and MS. Sojin Ouh for their clever and catchy design of the curriculum. My gratitude also goes to those who supported this work with their generous endorsements.

Above all, I express my deepest gratitude to my co-writers Kil Jae Park (and his wife Jee Young and children Jeremy and Daniel), Kevin Park (and his wife Irene, and children Jubilee, Emily, and Natalie), and my wife Jackie (and my two sons, Jonathan and David) whose deep affection for and dedication to Korean American youths made this journey exciting and fruitful.

Hak Joon Lee

iDenti
slide to unlock

LESSON 1
Banana?!

How Banana Are You?

(15 Minutes)

Here is a quick questionnaire to see how Korean or American you are. Circle the answer for each question below. Remember that this questionnaire is not scientifically proven and is never meant to be right/better or wrong/worse. Feel free to discuss your answers with each other.

Your church senior pastor walks in the door. What do you do?

Bow and say, "An yung ha se yo?"

Say, "Hi, pastor"

Your friend is taking you out to eat. If givien a choice, you would prefer to go to a...

American Restaurant

You won a vacation package to Hawaii and you are allowed to take one friend with you. You would take...

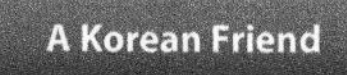

A Non-Korean Friend

When parents are not present, young siblings should listen to older siblings

I watch Korean drama or listen to Korean music at least once a week	Agree	Disagree
You sprained your ankle in a soccer game. You would prefer to see	An Acupuncturist	Medical Doctor
It is important to obey your parents even if you disagree with them (i.e. choosing college or going to church).	Agree	Disagree
It is important to give a Korean name to addition to an American name to our children (given that you are married to another Korean American)	Agree	Disagree
Academic excellence is prerequisite for a successful life	Agree	Disagree
Parental approval is important when it comes to deciding my marriage	Agree	Disagree

News Feed

15 minutes

Born in the US
A Korean mother's son
Not white but yellow
A questioned identity
Needless angst and doubt
Against myself I struggle

Two separate worlds
Why must there be a conflict?
Is a choice required?
Not if I know my own heart
Korean or not
You know, I am a... Banana. -[1]

Grace came to America with her family when she was nine years old. She grew up in a Korean American church in Chicago with her Korean American friends. She loved everything Korean. By the time she was a High School junior she was really into "Hallyu," the Korean wave. She kept up her Korean language, reading Korean novels and manga. She really wanted to visit Korea and, after high school, she had an opportunity to go there with a few of her friends in a cultural exchange program. In Korea she felt at home. Grace had an "Ah ha!" experience there. She connected with Korea. She felt that she belonged there in a strong way. These were "her people." She felt that she was more Korean than American. She wanted to be "fully Korean" like her brothers and sisters in Korea. But during her trip she began to feel that the Korean people treated her with kindness but as a foreigner, a gyopo. She began to realize that Korea was a great place to visit as her home away from home but she could not live there as her true home. She began to understand that she was more Americanized than she realized. She began to question her identity more seriously. After she came back from the trip she had an opportunity to debrief her experience with some of her friends. Grace and her friends realized more clearly what it meant to be neither Korean nor American but Korean American.

---

[1] Ted Cho, "Who Doesn't Love Bananas" in *Who Doesn't Love Bananas: Collection of Immigrant Stories.*

Chat

1 What does the poem mean by "banana"? Can you give some examples of this?

2 What is the author trying to say in this poem?

3 How well does this poem and the story of Grace reflect your experience as a Korean American? Do you consider yourself more American than Korean or more Korean than American? Why?

4 Do you consider yourself Korean American? What does this mean to you?

Focus

All Americans are people with various cultural backgrounds (Italian American, African American, German American, Irish American, Korean American, Chinese American etc.). This means that every American is a bicultural (or multicultural) person whether one recognizes this or not. Koreans are no exception. Korean Americans are neither Koreans living in America nor Americans without any cultural heritage. Korean Americans, as bicultural people, are those who are fully American with their own unique Korean cultural heritage.

Text

20 minutes

Genesis 41:45-52

45 Pharaoh gave Joseph the name Zaphenath-Paneah and gave him
Asenath daughter of Potiphera, priest of On, to be his wife. And Joseph
went throughout the land of Egypt. **46** Joseph was thirty years old when
he entered the service of Pharaoh king of Egypt. And Joseph went out from
Pharaoh's presence and traveled throughout Egypt. **47** During the seven
years of abundance the land produced plentifully. **48** Joseph collected all
the food produced in those seven years of abundance in Egypt and stored
it in the cities. In each city he put the food grown in the fields surrounding
it. **49** Joseph stored up huge quantities of grain, like the sand of the sea;
it was so much that he stopped keeping records because it was beyond
measure. **50** Before the years of famine came, two sons were born to
Joseph by Asenath daughter of Potiphera, priest of On. **51** Joseph named
his firstborn Manasseh and said, "It is because God has made me forget all
my trouble and all my father's household." **52** The second son he named
Ephraim and said, "It is because God has made me fruitful in the land of my
suffering."

Daniel 1:3-9

3 Then the king ordered Ashpenaz, chief of his court officials, to bring in
some of the Israelites from the royal family and the nobility-- 4 young men
without any physical defect, handsome, showing aptitude for every kind
of learning, well informed, quick to understand, and qualified to serve in
the king's palace. He was to teach them the language and literature of the
Babylonians. 5 The king assigned them a daily amount of food and wine
from the king's table. They were to be trained for three years, and after that
they were to enter the king's service. 6 Among these were some from Judah:
Daniel, Hananiah, Mishael and Azariah. 7 The chief official gave them new
names: to Daniel, the name Belteshazzar; to Hananiah, Shadrach; to Mishael,
Meshach; and to Azariah, Abednego. 8 But Daniel resolved not to defile
himself with the royal food and wine, and he asked the chief official for
permission not to defile himself this way. 9 Now God had caused the official
to show favor and sympathy to Daniel,

Although Joseph achieved great stature in Egyptian society he never forgot that he was a Jew or where he came from. In fact, even though he was married to an Egyptian priestess, he gave his two sons the Hebrew names Ephraim and Manasseh.

Scan

1 In what ways were Joseph and Daniel bicultural? Identify/describe their characteristics based on the scripture.
(* See above Commentary on Joseph)

2 How did Joseph and Daniel attempt to retain their cultural heritage? How did they accommodate dominant cultures (Egyptian/Babylonian) within them?

3 In your opinion how did God use their bicultural backgrounds to achieve His plan? Please feel free to make use of stories of other figures in the Bible (e.g., Moses) to answer this question.

Message

Both Joseph and Daniel were bicultural and minorities in a dominant culture. This bicultural reality created for them a unique opportunity to serve God and humanity. Their faith enabled them to navigate between the two cultures in a way that faithfully witnessed to God's sovereignty. Knowing more than one culture enables us to get a deeper understanding of God and God's action in history.

Download & Apply

15 Minutes

1 In what ways are you bicultural? What do you think are the advantages of being bicultural? For example, what kind of practical advantages do you think are there for being able to speak two different languages fluently, i.e., Korean and English? (examples: dating, getting a job, college admission, enjoying mass media-drama and music)

2 What are some of the ways that we can develop or deepen our "bicultural-ness?"

3 In what ways can God use you because of your bicultural-ness? Discuss this in light of other bicultural people in the Scripture (e.g., Moses, Paul, Esther, etc.).

LESSON 2

"Go Back to Your Country!"

News Feed

15 minutes

James is a Korean American in his mid-thirties, working as an engineer and living in Atlanta. He was born and grew up in a predominantly white suburb in Boston. He has a painful memory of his early school years. In fourth grade, on his way back home from school, several large boys took him aside into an alley, and forced him to open his eyes as wide as he could. Showing a tiny pin in front of his eyes, they mockingly asked whether he could see it. It was a humiliating, never forgotten, experience. He grew up believing that slanted eyes are not as attractive as round and big eyes, and that yellow skin is less desirable than white. James believed that Caucasian features looked more "cool" and dignified than those of Asians. Another incident was when he ran into fights with others, he heard them shouting, "Go back to Korea!" Even in his adult life, he was often asked, "Where are you from?" until he finally would say his parents came from Korea.

In April 2007 a terrible tragedy took place at Virginia Tech University. A Korean American student, Seung Heui Cho, shot and killed 32 people. The whole nation was shocked by this senseless crime. The Korean American community was especially affected. Mary, a second generation Korean American teenager, took the news in stride. "What a shocking tragedy!" she thought. She felt terrible for the victims and their families. She also felt for the sister of the gunman and his parents. But she didn't associate herself with the gunman in anyway. She thought to herself, "After all, it is a total coincidence that the shooter happened to be a Korean American. This is an isolated incident and has nothing to do with me." But when she was at school, opening her locker, she heard a comment from some students who passed by her, "You crazy Koreans!" She turned around and could not identify who said it but she felt as though all eyes were on her. She felt isolated, lonely, and, for reasons that she did not even know, ashamed. For the first time in her life she felt like she was an outsider, a non-American.

Chat

1 Share your own personal stories and experiences about racism or racial discrimination, if you have any. Have you ever been teased and taunted with racial slurs? What were they, where did they happen, how did you respond, and how do you feel about them now?

2 Have you heard of other stories of racial discriminations against Asian Americans from someone you know?

3 Why do you think racism exists? What do you think is the source of racism?

4 Why is racism wrong?

Focus

Despite the progress made in the past several decades, racism still exists in America. Like air, it is an invisible social force that deeply affects our life. Racism is not just simple prejudice. Racism, according to Joseph Barndt, a Lutheran pastor and expert on this subject, is prejudice plus power. The first component of racism is racial prejudice– distorted, and biased views about people of different race. Yet prejudice alone does not make racism. Racism happens when prejudice is backed up by power (political, economic, social, cultural, and legal). Although we all have some form of distorted views or stereotypes about people of other races, it does not constitute racism. Racism takes place through the power that socially enforces racial prejudices as normative social expectations and behaviors for the whole society, usually for the advantage of a dominant race. In the United States one cannot deny that whites, who still hold the power, set most of the social and cultural standards to which, knowingly or unknowingly, we as minorities are pressured to fit.

In the following story of Mordecai and Haman in the book of Esther, we will examine more closely how racism operates through prejudice and power.

Text

20 minutes

Esther 3: 1-15

1 After these events, King Xerxes honored Haman son of Hammedatha, the
Agagite, elevating him and giving him a seat of honor higher than that of all
the other nobles. **2** All the royal officials at the king's gate knelt down and
paid honor to Haman, for the king had commanded this concerning him.
But Mordecai would not kneel down or pay him honor. **3** Then the royal
officials at the king's gate asked Mordecai, "Why do you disobey the king's
command?" **4** Day after day they spoke to him but he refused to comply.

Therefore they told Haman about it to see whether Mordecai's behavior would be tolerated, for he had told them he was a Jew. **5** When Haman saw that Mordecai would not kneel down or pay him honor, he was enraged. **6** Yet having learned who Mordecai's people were, he scorned the idea of killing only Mordecai. Instead Haman looked for a way to destroy all Mordecai's people, the Jews, throughout the whole kingdom of Xerxes. **7** In the twelfth year of King Xerxes, in the first month, the month of Nisan, they cast the pur (that is, the lot) in the presence of Haman to select a day and month. And the lot fell on the twelfth month, the month of Adar. **8** Then Haman said to King Xerxes, "There is a certain people dispersed and scattered among the peoples in all the provinces of your kingdom whose customs are different from those of all other people and who do not obey the king's laws; it is not in the king's best interest to tolerate them. **9** If it pleases the king, let a decree be issued to destroy them, and I will put ten thousand talents of silver into the royal treasury for the men who carry out this business." **10** So the king took his signet ring from his finger and gave it to Haman son of Hammedatha, the Agagite, the enemy of the Jews. **11** "Keep the money," the king said to Haman, "and do with the people as you please." **12** Then on the thirteenth day of the first month the royal secretaries were summoned. They wrote out in the script of each province and in the language of each people all Haman's orders to the king's satraps, the governors of the various provinces and the nobles of the various peoples. These were written in the name of King Xerxes himself and sealed with his own ring. 13 Dispatches were sent by couriers to all the king's provinces with the order to destroy, kill and annihilate all the Jews-- young and old, women and little children-- on a single day, the thirteenth day of the twelfth month, the month of Adar, and to plunder their goods. 14 A copy of the text of the edict was to be issued as law in every province and made known to the people of every nationality so they would be ready for that day. 15 Spurred on by the king's command, the couriers went out, and the edict was issued in the citadel of Susa. The king and Haman sat down to drink, but the city of Susa was bewildered.

This is a fascinating story. If you want to know how this story turns out read Esther chapters 4 through 6.

Scan

1 Why did Mordecai and the Israelites face the danger of genocide in Persia? What had Mordecai and Israelites done wrong? Do you think that Mordecai's refusal to bow down and pay honor to Haman (v.2) deserve genocide?

2 Read chapter 3:6. Comment on Haman's decision to destroy all the Jews based upon Mordecai's action. What do you find to be irrational and extreme about Haman's decision? Can you think of some reasons why Haman would make such a decision? (See 3:8)

3 In the context of chapter 3, verse 8, discuss how a minority culture and customs are stereotyped and treated as inferior, and a nuisance or even a threat to the majority. Are different customs (e.g., eating kimchi, speaking Korean in public places, or wearing Korean traditional costumes, etc.) bad things?

4 What did Mordecai and Esther do to avoid genocide? What can we learn from them?

Message

As in the time of Mordecai and Esther, genocides are an ever-threatening reality in many parts of the world like Rwanda, Bosnia and Sudan. These experiences of genocides and violence around the world are the result of fear, hatred, and a sense of threat that a dominant group of people have against a minority group with different cultural and ethnic backgrounds. Even in the United States we have a very long and painful history of racism and discrimination against minority people. The enslavement of Africans, the massacre of Native Americans, the internment of Japanese Americans during World War II are among the well-known examples. Even now, in the United States, people are discriminated against because of their cultural and racial differences. Racism is wrong because it is against God's intention for humanity. God created all people in God's image to be free and equal. Discriminating against others because of their race and culture is offensive to God; it not only violates the image of God created in them but also frustrates the fulfillment of their God given potentials. Therefore racial discrimination is sin.

Download & Apply

15 minutes

1 How should we Christians treat people of different races and culture? What are some ways that we, intentionally or unintentionally, discriminate against others because of their race and culture?

2 Leviticus 19:33-34 reads as follows: "When an alien resides with you in your land, you shall not oppress the alien. The alien who resides with you shall be to you as the citizen among you; you shall love the alien as yourself, for you were aliens in the land of Egypt: I am the LORD your God." How does this passage speak to Korean Americans?

3 When we experience racism, how can we respond? What can we, as church and community, do to prevent and fight against racism? What can we learn from other communities, such as African Americans and Jewish Americans regarding their struggle against discrimination and racism?

Did U Know?

Forever Foreigners?: Snapshots of Racism in America

Although the US society has made an impressive stride in the area of racial equality, as indicated by the election of Barack Obama as the 44th President, and racism is not as blatant as it used to be, racism still exists in various and subtle forms. Asian Americans continue to face institutional and cultural forms of racism on a daily basis. Here are some of the snapshots of racism that Asian Americans continue to experience in the American society today.

- Throughout the US history, Asian Americans have been portrayed as "forever foreigners" regardless of their citizenship and duration of residence in the US. No matter how long they have lived here and how fluently they speak English, they are often treated as outsiders who do not belong in the US.

- The majority of non-Asian Americans are not able to make a distinction between Korean Americans and other Asian American groups, treating all as one generic, ethnic group. About 28 percent of non-Asian Americans say that they rarely or never interact with Asian Americans.

- Many of non-Asian Americans believe that Asian Americans do not face any form of racism/discrimination at all. Racism is regarded as a Black and White issue. The stereotype of Asian Americans as model minority exaggerates their success, hiding the discriminations they face in the US.

- Despite the approximately 60,000 Asian Americans serving in active duty in the U.S. Armed Services, there still exists a high level of suspicion about the loyalty of Asian Americans. About 45 percent of the general population believe that Asian Americans are more loyal to their countries of ancestry than to the United States.

- Asian Americans are severely underrepresented in leadership positions in corporations, colleges, and federal government. They have respectively a 55%, 41%, and 30% chance to be promoted to the managerial level in corporations, colleges and federal government when compared to the national average. For Caucasian Americans, the percentage is 120%, 130% and 130% respectively (when 100% is considered a national average).

- Out of some 3,200 college presidents in the United States, there are only 33 Asian Americans, including Dr. Jim Yong Kim of Dartmouth College in this position.

---

source: http://www.sdnn.com/sandiego/2009-05-13/news/economy/report-racism-towards-asian-americans-persists##ixzz0aqcmiW9i

LESSON 3

The Broken Heroes

News Feed

15 minutes

My family immigrated to Flushing, NY when I was nine years old. I remember the plane ride well. It was Japanese Airlines. I remember because my father spoke Japanese to the flight attendants. I didn't know that my father could speak Japanese. When we arrived at New York's JFK airport my father asked for directions in English. I also didn't know that he could speak English. I thought he was pretty cool for being able speak in English as well as in Japanese. Hey, this was my dad. But when I later learned to speak English fluently, I realized how broken my father's English really was. In fact, as I became more "Americanized," I realized how painfully Korean my father really was. He didn't seem so cool anymore.

He got a job as a commercial artist in some company and every day when he came home from work he was just in a bad mood and brought the whole family down. I began to resent him. Then one day he called home and asked me to bring his wallet to work because he forgot it. So I went there and walked into this large room with a maze of cubicles. I had trouble finding him. He was tucked away, way at the corner, with what seemed like the smallest space there. I gave him the wallet and he said, "Tim, let's go out, I'll buy you lunch." So I followed him out but on the way he stopped at an office. The door was open and as we approached it I heard a couple of people talking and laughing aloud in there, just having a good time. My father stopped at the doorway. He didn't go in, and I stood beside him. We waited there standing for some time. This manager guy finally noticed us, immediately stopped laughing, turned to my father and said, what sounded like a snarl, "What do you want!" My father, in his painfully broken English said, "I go for lunch now. This is my number one son, Tim." He said it with anticipation. He was introducing me to his boss. I was embarrassed. The man didn't even glance at me. He blurted out, "Well, you better be back in thirty minutes!"

My father's eyes dropped. He didn't look at me. He couldn't look at me. We stood there together, silent, awkward. It seemed like a long time. The men turned and continued their conversation and laughter. At that moment I felt rage and shame at the same time. Part of me wanted to go over there and punch this guy out. How dare he treat us like that. How dare he speak to my father like that! But I didn't do anything. I didn't say anything. I just stood there feeling really small and helpless. My father walked out and I followed. I don't remember what we had for lunch that day but I do remember not saying anything as we ate. I understood him after that, why he was in a bad mood when he came home. I understood what he was enduring every day but couldn't share with us. My father who had his small but respectable art business in Korea with several apprentices under him was going through this every day. I had new respect for my father. Although we never spoke about the incident, I connected with him that day. I understood. I thought he was cool once again. He was my dad!

Chat

1 What do you think Tim felt at the office witnessing how his father was treated?

2 Have you ever been ashamed of /embarrassed by your parents because of their cultural differences (e.g., food, language/accent, job, outlook, social manners…)?

3 In the story, Tim felt embarrassed by his father, but at the same time he was able to understand what his father was going through every day. Have you ever had a similar experience through which you were able to understand your parents more deeply?

Focus

The feeling of shame, rebellion, and pressure to distance one's self from parents is found in every culture and society. In an immigrant situation, this problem is made worse due to a more severe cultural and generational gap between parents and youth. Sometimes, though, children fail to appreciate what immigrant parents endure in order to provide for the family and rarely do parents share their hardship with their children. Often the result is the emotional disconnect and misunderstanding between parents and children. Following is the story of Joseph, the Prime Minister of Egypt, who found himself caught between his immigrant Hebrew family and Egyptian culture.

Text

20 minutes

Joseph was the eleventh son of Jacob. Jacob had a special love for Joseph because he was "the son of his old age" (Gen. 37:3). When his brothers saw that Jacob loved Joseph more than all his brothers, they hated him. When Joseph was seventeen, his brothers betrayed him and sold him to Egypt as a slave. However, God was with Joseph and Joseph eventually became the person in charge of Egypt, second to Pharaoh in power. After he came into power in Egypt, he was once again reunited with his brothers and his father Jacob. After being reunited with his family, Joseph reveals to Pharaoh about his family background as being shepherds and wins Pharaoh's approval and provision for his family. Considering that shepherds were despised in the Egyptian culture as being uncivilized, revealing his family background to Pharaoh was a very bold and remarkable action by Joseph that deserves our attention. Would you have done the same if you were Joseph?

Genesis 46:26 – 47:6

26 All those who went to Egypt with Jacob-- those who were his direct descen-
dants, not counting his sons' wives-- numbered sixty-six persons. 27 With the
two sons who had been born to Joseph in Egypt, the members of Jacob's family,
which went to Egypt, were seventy in all. 28 Now Jacob sent Judah ahead of
him to Joseph to get directions to Goshen. When they arrived in the region of
Goshen, 29 Joseph had his chariot made ready and went to Goshen to meet his
father Israel. As soon as Joseph appeared before him, he threw his arms around
his father and wept for a long time. 30 Israel said to Joseph, "Now I am ready to
die, since I have seen for myself that you are still alive." 31 Then Joseph said to
his brothers and to his father's household, "I will go up and speak to Pharaoh
and will say to him, 'My brothers and my father's household, who were living
in the land of Canaan, have come to me. 32 The men are shepherds; they tend
livestock, and they have brought along their flocks and herds and everything
they own.' 33 When Pharaoh calls you in and asks, 'What is your occupation?'
34 you should answer, 'Your servants have tended livestock from our boyhood
on, just as our fathers did.' Then you will be allowed to settle in the region of
Goshen, for all shepherds are detestable to the Egyptians." Genesis 47:1 Joseph
went and told Pharaoh, "My father and brothers, with their flocks and herds
and everything they own, have come from the land of Canaan and are now in
Goshen." 2 He chose five of his brothers and presented them before Pharaoh. 3
Pharaoh asked the brothers, "What is your occupation?" "Your servants are shepherds," they replied to Pharaoh, "just as our fathers were." 4 They also said to him,
"We have come to live here awhile, because the famine is severe in Canaan and
your servants' flocks have no pasture. So now, please let your servants settle in
Goshen." 5 Pharaoh said to Joseph, "Your father and your brothers have come to
you, 6 and the land of Egypt is before you; settle your father and your brothers in
the best part of the land. Let them live in Goshen. And if you know of any among
them with special ability, put them in charge of my own livestock."

Scan

1 How would you feel if you were in Joseph's position and learned that shepherds (the occupation of his parents) are detestable to Egyptians?

2 What do you think was Joseph's challenge/struggle in sharing his father's background with Pharaoh?

3 Do you think Joseph's action in revealing his Hebrew parents' background was an honorable and courageous thing to do? What would you have done if you were in Joseph's position? Why or why not?

Message

All parents are imperfect, and many are also struggling and broken. But despite their brokenness and imperfection, one thing is clear: *They love us and do their best to provide for the family, sometimes even at the cost of risking their own careers and well-being.* It is for this reason that Ephesians 6:1 tells us that it is our Christian calling to honor our parents in the Lord. Joseph is a good example for us as he continued to honor and care for his father in a culture that looked down upon his father's culture and livelihood.

Download & Apply

15 minutes

1 What can we do to express our appreciation to our parents or to show our parents that we honor them? [e.g., Send them a card, write a letter or email, cook them a meal, help with house chores, obey them for one day no matter what the cost may be…]

2 Reaching out to our parents in an attempt to get a deeper understanding of who they are, including their struggles and needs, is something that we do as Christians. Consider the following suggestions: Ask your parents out for a drive or take them out for coffee and ask them to tell you the story of their courtship -- how they met each other and married; ask them what it was like when they first came to the U.S. and what difficulties they faced then, what difficulties they face now, and so on….

A Letter to My Parent(s)

Dear ________,

LESSON

Is it Wrong to Be Different?

News Feed

15 minutes

Wendy is a young girl who goes to a school where most of the students are white. She feels the pressure to blend in and she tries to convince herself that she is not really that different from her white peers. For example, she always paid special attention to her appearance in order to fit in more closely with her Caucasian friends. She also felt very self-conscious and expressed dissatisfaction with her slight accent. One day, her teacher invited her mother to come and share aspects of Korean culture and history to her class. When Wendy found this out, she was a bit nervous and even embarrassed. What would her friends think? She thought. How would her mother be accepted by her friends? And would her presentation of the Korean culture just emphasize Wendy's difference from the rest of the class? Wendy was worried that this whole thing could sabotage all of her efforts to fit in with her white friends. The day finally came and she sat nervously in her seat as her mother began her presentation. At first, Wendy was more attentive to the reactions of her class than to her mother's presentation. Then as the presentation went on, she discovered that her friends were actually enjoying the presentation. And she was even surprised to find that she, too, was learning new things about Korea and its culture. For example, she learned that Koreans invented the first printing press centuries before Gutenberg. She also learned that the Korean alphabet is one of the most scientifically designed languages in the world and that kim-chi was considered by Time magazine as one of the eight healthiest foods in the world. After the presentation, many of her friends came to her and told her that her mom did a great job. Even after that day, many of her friends approached her with other questions about Korean culture. This experience gave her a renewed interest in her cultural heritage. For the first time, Wendy felt proud of her Korean cultural heritage and thought about what it would be like to visit Korea someday.

Chat

1 Why do you think that Wendy felt the pressure to blend in and deny the differences that she had as a Korean American? Have you ever felt a similar pressure in your own life?

2 Is being culturally different necessarily a bad thing? Why or why not?

3 What do you see to be the main differences between Korean and American culture? Grab someone near you and as you talk, write down your answers in your student book.

4 Which aspects of Korean culture do you want to affirm and celebrate? Why?

Focus

Korean Americans feel a great pressure to conform to the dominant Caucasian culture at the expense of suppressing or even rejecting their Korean cultural heritage. In essence, this pressure usually leads Korean Americans to view their cultural differences as deficit rather than as gifts. Unfortunately, some Christians have argued that Christian faith erases cultural differences and uniqueness, but the following Biblical text (and others) challenges such misunderstanding.

Text

15 minutes

Revelation 7:9-10

9 After this I looked and there before me was a great multitude that no one
could count, from every nation, tribe, people and language, standing before
the throne and in front of the Lamb. They were wearing white robes and were
holding palm branches in their hands. 10 And they cried out in a loud voice:
"Salvation belongs to our God, who sits on the throne, and to the Lamb."

Scan

1 According to this text, what do you think the Kingdom of God will look like? Why?

2 Why does the writer of Revelation (John of Patmos) define the multitude more specifically as those from "every nation, tribe, people and language"? What do you think is the significance of these distinctions?

3 Can you think of other biblical passages that affirm diversity?

The word "nations" in Greek is a derivation of the word "ethnos" from which we get the English word "ethnicity." This suggests that the Kingdom of God will be made up of all kinds of people from every ethnic group and language.

Message

Frequently, Christians think that Christian faith removes/erases all cultural differences among people. According to the passage in Revelation, however, the Kingdom of God reflects the diversity of people from every nation and from every language group praising the glory of God in unity. This understanding is important for us in that it challenges the domination of people by one culture and lifts up every culture as an inherent part of God's creation. This understanding provides the strength and confidence for Korean Americans to embrace and celebrate their cultural differences and uniqueness. This understanding also challenges us to respect and celebrate other cultures as God's gifts to all of humanity.

Korean Waves

refers to the significantly increased popularity of South Korean culture around the world

Download & Apply

20 minutes

1. Make a banner that celebrates the cultural heritage of Korean Americans (e.g., food, clothing, lifestyle, language…etc).

2. Have you ever seen a Korean movie or drama? Discuss what is different about this movie or drama from American movies or dramas. Did you notice any distinctive cultural characteristics in these movies or dramas?

3. Share with your group "something Korean" that you really enjoy doing/eating/seeing/hearing, etc., and why.

4. What activities can you do either as an individual or as a group at school, church or home to celebrate Korean culture? Are you aware of any Korean cultural celebrations in your neighborhood that you can take part in?

Did u know?

World's Healthiest Foods: Kimchi (Korea)

Did you know that Kimchi was picked as one of five healthiest foods in the world by Health Magazine in 2006? Believe it or not, Koreans eat about 40 pounds of kimchi per person each year. The reddish fermented cabbage (and sometimes radish) dish—made with a mix of garlic, salt, vinegar, chile peppers, and other spices—is served at every meal, either alone or mixed with rice or noodles. And it's part of a high-fiber, low-fat diet that has kept obesity at bay in Korea. Kimchi also is used in everything from soups to pancakes, and as a topping on pizza and burgers.

FYI, Kimchi (or kimchee) is loaded with vitamins A, B, and C, but its biggest benefit may be in its "healthy bacteria" called lactobacilli, found in fermented foods like kimchi and yogurt. According to a recent study, this good bacteria found in kimchi has been known to help with digestion, and even prevent some infections in our body. And more good news: Some studies have shown that fermented cabbage has compounds that may prevent the growth of cancer. What were the other four world's healthiest foods? Olive Oil (Spain), Soy (Japan), Yogurt (Greece), and Lentil (India). For further information, see Health Magazine, March 2006.

http://www.koreanbeacon.com/wp-content/uploads/2009/05/kimchi.jpg

The Korean American Cultural Heritage Flag Template

Directions: Using a separate piece of construction paper (minimum: letter size), draw one of the templates below to fill the whole page. Cut out the shapes and fill it with drawings, writings or both that describe the uniqueness of Korean American cultural heritage. Using a string, weave the flags (shapes) of your group together hang it in your room as a way of celebrating the uniqueness of Korean American culture.

e.g.,

LESSON

In Your Own Words

News Feed

15 minutes

John went to church with his parents ever since he was an infant. He grew up attending Sunday school, learning Bible lessons and getting involved with church activities. He had friends in the church and attended most of the church events and went to church retreats. As a kid he participated in church choirs and Christmas pageants. He regularly memorized Bible verses as assigned by his Sunday school teachers and his parents.

In high school John began to resent the fact that he had to go to church every Sunday, now "forced" by his parents. He wanted to do other things on Sundays. He still came to church and enjoyed it from time to time but his resentment also came and went from time to time. Eventually John graduated from high school and went away to college. It was the first time that he was away from his family and he felt free from their control. He wanted to shed his old self and wanted to blend in with his new environment and his new friends. Church was one of the first things to go. He didn't look for a church or attend a Christian fellowship in college. John slept in on Sundays and church became a distant memory for him. When he came home for the holidays he attended his home church but it was different. He felt "out of it" and a bit "weird" being in church again. Some parts were familiar and gave him good feelings but he felt out of place. Next time he came home he gave excuses to his parents that he was too tired to go to church and he needed to catch up on his sleep from studying from school. One Sunday morning his father confronted him and demanded that he get dressed to go to church with him. John could not take it anymore. He shouted, "Don't shove your church on me! I'm tired of it!" That put a strain on his relationship with his father. Slowly his parents got used to John not attending church even when he came home. John drifted away from the church life and faith.

"Silent Exodus"

Large numbers of Korean American youths participate actively in church life through their youth groups. They attend Sunday worship services, Bible studies, prayer meetings, small group discussions, fellowships, mission projects, retreats as well as many other events and activities. However, after high school, most of these youths stop attending church and many drift away from the faith. Some have estimated that the majority of the once church-attending Korean Americans stop attending church sometime in their college and post-college years. This phenomenon has been termed as the "silent exodus."

Chat

1 Can you relate to John's drifting away from church and faith? Do you know of friends who have gone through a similar process?

2 Would you continue to attend the church worship and remain active in the church life after you graduate from high school if there is no one to force you to go to church? Why or why not?

3 Have you ever heard of the "Silent Exodus" before? Why do you think the "Silent Exodus" happens?

Focus

Korean American churches provide fellowship, friends, and community for Korean American youths. This is an important part of the Korean American experience. However, one of the reasons young people, who were once very active in church life, leave church after high school is that their faiths have been largely "second-hand." Many come to church because of the insistence of their parents and go through the "motions" of church but too often the youths do not get to the point where genuine confession of faith in Jesus Christ is made and nurtured. The following passage teaches us not only the importance of true confession of faith but also the importance of discipleship that must follow after we receive Christ as our Lord and Savior.

Text

15 minutes

Matt. 16:13-26

13 When Jesus came to the region of Caesarea Philippi, he asked his disciples,
"Who do people say the Son of Man is?" 14 They replied, "Some say John the
Baptist; others say Elijah; and still others, Jeremiah or one of the prophets."
15 "But what about you?" he asked. "Who do you say I am?" 16 Simon Peter
answered, "You are the Christ, the Son of the living God." 17 Jesus replied,
"Blessed are you, Simon son of Jonah, for this was not revealed to you by man,
but by my Father in heaven. 18 And I tell you that you are Peter, and on this
rock I will build my church, and the gates of Hades will not overcome it. 19 I
will give you the keys of the kingdom of heaven; whatever you bind on earth
will be bound in heaven, and whatever you loose on earth will be loosed in
heaven." 20 Then he warned his disciples not to tell anyone that he was the
Christ. 21 From that time on Jesus began to explain to his disciples that he
must go to Jerusalem and suffer many things at the hands of the elders, chief

priests and teachers of the law, and that he must be killed and on the third
day be raised to life. 22 Peter took him aside and began to rebuke him.
"Never, Lord!" he said. "This shall never happen to you!" 23 Jesus turned
and said to Peter, "Get behind me, Satan! You are a stumbling block to me;
you do not have in mind the things of God, but the things of men." 24 Then
Jesus said to his disciples, "If anyone would come after me, he must deny
himself and take up his cross and follow me. 25 For whoever wants to save
his life will lose it, but whoever loses his life for me will find it. 26 What
good will it be for a man if he gains the whole world, yet forfeits his soul?
Or what can a man give in exchange for his soul?

Scan

1 What are the two questions that Jesus asks the disciples? How are these two questions different from one another? Which question do you think was harder for the disciples to answer and why?

2 If Jesus were to ask you, "Who do you say that I am?", how would you answer?

3 Why do you think it's important that we confess Jesus to be the Christ for ourselves rather than having a "borrowed" or "second-hand" faith that merely repeats what other people have said?

Message

In this biblical text we can outline two different ways of practicing the Christian faith. The first way is simply repeating what others say about Jesus. This is largely a second-hand or borrowed faith without any personal conviction. It was easy for the disciples to repeat what other people were saying about Jesus when Jesus asked them, "Who do people say that the Son of Man is?" People who have been going to church for many years could still be just repeating what others are saying about Jesus without having personal conviction or relationship with Jesus. Sure, they may be saying the right words but their confession can be empty of faith. The second way is personally confessing Jesus as the Christ or Messiah, God's Son and our Lord and Savior as Peter did. Until we receive Jesus for ourselves, Christian faith will never be real. Real faith is knowing Christ and having a relationship with Him, not merely knowing about Christ.

Download & Apply

25 minutes

1 Where are you in your faith journey? Take a few minutes to complete "My Creed of Faith" that is included at the end of this chapter. If you have not yet made a personal confession of faith, take time to write down some of the questions that you have about Christian faith (Use the next page).

2 Express your faith through one of these methods:
   1) Write a poem
   2) Draw a picture/painting
   3) Write a song
   4) Method of your choice

My Creed of Faith

Please take time to write up your own creed of Christian faith based on your own understanding and conviction about God, Jesus Christ, the Holy Spirit and the Church. You are not asked to write an eloquent creed of faith but a genuine and personal expression of faith and understanding. Whenever possible, use common words to describe your faith. Be creative and feel free to use metaphors and images to articulate your faith. Please understand that this is YOUR understanding of faith. Therefore, your creed of faith probably will be different from others. Feel free to be YOU.

I believe in God.….

And in Jesus Christ….

And in the Holy Spirit

And in the Church

LESSON 6
No Matter What!

News Feed

15 minutes

I reached out for my cell phone to text message Jay, my best friend who is also a member of the gang Korean Power. I needed a person to share my frustration with after a huge confrontation with my parents who kept getting on my case because of my school work. They just don't know me. They don't seem to care about what my interests in life and the struggles that I go through at school. Sometimes, I even wonder whether they really love me anymore. They seem to be more concerned about my grades than how I feel. Why couldn't they see that I am different from my sister who is a sophomore in Harvard? I hate studying, but they think that I will be a total failure if I don't do well at school. I really don't care about becoming a doctor or a lawyer. Why can't they see that my passion is football? In all honesty, I hate school. I hate being treated like a foreigner and as if I'm nobody. People don't have any respect for me and my feelings. Sometimes, I wonder if things would be different if I were a white person. I don't particularly enjoy what I do when I get together with the guys in Korean Power. But they seem to be the only people who accept me as who I am and understand my struggles. "C U @ BK @ 9. gotta talk."

Chat

1 What is going on with this character (who is texting with Jay)? What pressure is the character experiencing at home and at school?

2 What do you think this character is longing for? And is this longing something that is common in many others?

3 Can you relate to the experience of this character? If you were his close friend, how would you help him to deal with his frustrations?

4 Do you think his involvement with the gang provides a true answer to his needs and problems? Why or why not?

Focus

There is within every one of us a deep longing to be accepted and respected as an individual with his/her own uniqueness. For this reason, when one is not accepted as who he/she is without condition, the pain and discouragement can be very real and deep even if the person is not able to articulate that experience well. And because the drive for acceptance and belonging is so great within us, people will go to extreme means to find that acceptance.

Text

20 minutes

Luke 19:1-10

1 Jesus entered Jericho and was passing through. 2 A man was there by the
name of Zacchaeus; he was a chief tax collector and was wealthy. 3 He wanted
to see who Jesus was, but being a short man he could not, because of the crowd.
4 So he ran ahead and climbed a sycamore-fig tree to see him, since Jesus was
coming that way. 5 When Jesus reached the spot, he looked up and said to him,
"Zacchaeus, come down immediately. I must stay at your house today." 6 So he
came down at once and welcomed him gladly. 7 All the people saw this and
began to mutter, "He has gone to be the guest of a 'sinner.'" 8 But Zacchaeus stood
up and said to the Lord, "Look, Lord! Here and now I give half of my possessions
to the poor, and if I have cheated anybody out of anything, I will pay back four
times the amount." 9 Jesus said to him, "Today salvation has come to this house,
because this man, too, is a son of Abraham. 10 For the Son of Man came to seek
and to save what was lost."

Romans 5:8

But God proves his love for us in that while we still were sinners Christ died for us.

Scan

1 What do you know about Zacchaeus? Why do you think people called Zacchaeus a sinner (v. 7) and how do you think people treated him?

2 What do you think is the significance of the fact that Zacchaeus climbed the sycamore tree? What does it say about the hidden need of Zacchaues?

3 What was so remarkable about Jesus' treatment of Zacchaeus?

4 What changes can you name in Zacchaeus after his encounter with Jesus? Why do you think these changes took place and what is the significance of this change?

Romans 5:8 tells us that "Christ died for us while we were yet sinners." This is to say that God's love for us never originated from our deeds or even our willingness to change for the better from our sinful ways. God chose to love us AS WE ARE independent of our actions and merits. If God loved us even when we were sinners, there is nothing that we can do to make God stop loving us. The understanding and acceptance of this love is powerful because it allows us to love ourselves as God loves us—as who we are with all our inadequacies and imperfections!

Message

God accepts us as who we are without any condition. The fact that Jesus died for us while we were still sinners proves this truth. God does not condone our sinful and immoral actions. And yet, God still loves us. God's love is not based on our merits. He loves us not because we are a certain kind of people or because we do certain kind of words but in spite of our failings, sins, problems, and brokenness. This understanding of God's unconditional love frees us from the anxiety and pressure to seek acceptance through our works and achievements.

Download & Apply

15 minutes

1 Share with your group any experience of unconditional love from someone in your life. (If you cannot think of a person, what experience can you share that most resembles unconditional love in your life?) What does the unconditional love of God mean for you in your life (i.e., at school, home, church and in friendships)?

2 How does the unconditional love of God help you to deal with your experience as an ethnic minority?

3 Using the form "The Covenant with the Self" write a personal contract that promises not to speak or think anything negative about yourself for a specified period of time (e.g., one week).

The Covenant With the Self

I, ____________________ hereby promise that I will not say any negative things about myself in any shape or form in any situation for a period of thirty calendar days*

signed on________ day of

month of ____________

in the year of______________

signed by (self)________________________

witness ________________________

* Every person must find a partner who can hold you accountable to your covenant. Both persons must sign the covenant form. Please note that the partner has to be of same gender or your teacher/Jundosanim. After signing this contract, every person must post the covenant form in a visible place in the person's room to serve as a reminder. A copy should be given to the partner/witness.

LESSON

My Spiritual Home

News Feed

15 minutes

Diary of a Korean American Teenage Girl:

Fri. Oct. 12

Dear diary,

Today's youth group at church was very special to me. Maybe it was because it was a tough week at school. I really hated school this week. I really felt like an alien.

I was so embarrassed in class when they discussed Asian American history. The teacher was lecturing about Korean history and someone blurted out, "Hey, I heard Koreans eat dogs." Kids laughed and few of them looked at me knowing that I was Korean. I felt very embarrassed and small. I forced myself to laugh with them but inside I felt like I was two different people. One person felt hurt and invisible. The other person desperately wanted to be accepted by the group.

At the youth group the praises and the sermon from my JDSN made me feel better. The prayer meeting was also great. I felt at home. I didn't have to hide or prove myself to anybody. I belonged there. My youth group is a sanctuary to me.

I shared what happened at school with my youth group and everyone understood exactly how I felt.

I thank God for my church. Although it is not always perfect, I really need it. I am glad there is a place for me to go where I am accepted.

Chat

1 Have you ever felt like the girl who wrote in her diary? Share freely.

2 Has your church life been helpful for you in dealing with your struggles? If so, how?

3 Why do you think many English-speaking Korean and Asian Americans still attend Korean and Asian American churches even when they could worship in other American churches?

Focus

Church is a spiritual home for many Korean Americans. For Korean Americans, church is more than a place to worship God just on Sundays. Church also provides a sense of safety and sanctuary for Korean Americans who often feel invisible or ignored in American society. This is why the percentage of Koreans attending church is much higher in North America (about 60%) compared to the Koreans in Korea (24%). Church is our place of refuge, where we can be accepted as who we are by God and others. Church is a place we can come always back to. In church we find caring support, healing of emotional wounds, and growth of our faiths. This is where we experience a sense of wholeness, which no other place provides.

Did U Know?

Top Ten Things About Korean American Churches

TEN

The first Korean American church, the Korean Methodist Mission Church, was found in 1903 in Hawai'i by the first group of immigrants from Korea.

NINE

It is the Korean Christian organization called The Korean Evangelical Society in San Francisco that published the very first Korean language newspaper in the U.S in 1906.

EIGHT

Korean American churches played a crucial role in fighting for the independence of Korea from Japan from 1910 to 1945 through raising funds for the "freedom fighters," educating the leaders, and organizing resistance groups.

SEVEN

Syngman Rhee (1875-1965), a leader in the Korean Independence Movement overseas and the first president of Korea, was an active lay leader of the Korean American church in Hawai'i.

SIX

The Korean American church is the place to go if you want to make new Korean American friends because 65%-70% of the Korean American population has membership in Korean American churches. (In Korea, only about 25% of the population see themselves as Christians)

FIVE

Korean American churches are indispensable for the life of Korean immigrants. In addition to religious services, they provide a place for social gathering, fellowship, exchange of helpful information and providing various kinds of social services such as interpretation, school registration, job search, finding apartments, caring for elderly, and visiting the sick.

FOUR

Had it not been for Korean language school programs in Korean American churches (and your loving parents who forced you to go to the school every Saturday), you would have a difficult time enjoying

THREE 원더걸스 그리고 소녀시대 today. (Did you know that 90% of Korean language programs in the US are offered by Korean American churches?) It is very likely that you will find your future spouse (if you are thinking about marrying another Korean American) in the Korean American church
TWO than any other place. (You might even get married in a Korean American church, too!)

You become leaders in Korean American churches. It is a natural place to
ONE develop your social and leadership skills (communication, organizational, and even financial management).

Free lunch (yeah, baby!) It's free and it also tastes good! Korean American churches know how to eat!

"There was not a needy person among them..." Acts 4:34

The earliest Christians were known by their close community where they tended to the needs of each other. They shared their possessions with one another and they prayed for one another. They cared for one another in costly ways without being a closed group (Acts 2:42-45). The early church grew rapidly because "day by day the Lord added to their number those who were being saved" (Acts 2:45).

Their way of life was so strikingly different from the way of life of their society that other people begin to notice them and wanted to know more about their faith. The way these early Christians lived together became a witness to Christ for others.

In the same way it is important to remember that we are called to love our brothers and sisters in Christ and tend to their needs in the church. We cannot be effective witnesses for Christ without taking care of one another. But taking care of Christians in the church does not mean we become an exclusive club, closed to the needs outside of the church. In fact, the opposite is true. As we take care of fellow Christians we are empowered to look outward to the needs of the poor and downtrodden outside of the church.

"Contribute to the needs of the saints; extend hospitality to strangers." Romans 12:13

Text

20 minutes

Ephesians 1:23

23 [the church] is his [Jesus Christ's] body, the fullness of him who fills all in all.

Ephesians 4:15-16

15 But speaking the truth in love, we must grow up in every way into him
who is the head, into Christ, 16 from whom the whole body, joined and knit
together by every ligament with which it is equipped, as each part is working
properly, promotes the body's growth in building itself up in love.

1 Corinthians 12:12-27

12 The body is a unit, though it is made up of many parts; and though all its
parts are many, they form one body. So it is with Christ. 13 For we were all
baptized by one Spirit into one body –whether Jews or Greeks, slave or free–
and we were all given the one Spirit to drink. 14 Now the body is not made up
of one part but of many. 15 If the foot should say, "Because I am not a hand, I
do not belong to the body," it would not for that reason cease to be part of the
body.

16 And if the ear should say, "Because I am not an eye, I do not belong to
the body," it would not for that reason cease to be part of the body. 17 If the
whole body were an eye, where would the sense of hearing be? If the whole
body were an ear, where would the sense of smell be? 18 But in fact God has
arranged the parts in the body, every one of them, just as he wanted them
to be. 19 If they were all one part, where would the body be? 20 As it is, there
are many parts, but one body. 21 The eye cannot say to the hand, "I don't
need you!" And the head cannot say to the feet, "I don't need you!" 22 On the
contrary, those parts of the body that seem to be weaker are indispensable,
23 and the parts that we think are less honorable we treat with special honor.
And the parts that are unpresentable are treated with special modesty, 24
while our presentable parts need no special treatment. But God has com-

bined the members of the body and has given greater honor to the parts that lacked it, 25 so that there should be no division in the body, but that its parts should have equal concern for each other. 26 If one part suffers, every part suffers with it; if one part is honored, every part rejoices with it. 27 Now you are the body of Christ, and each one of you is a part of it.

Scan

1 Apostle Paul uses the image of the human body (with Christ as its head) to describe the nature and function of the church. What do you think it means when we say that the church is the body of Christ? What do you think Paul wants us to learn about church from this metaphor?

2 Read verse 21 again. Paul is criticizing individualistic and self-sufficient attitudes in the church. In what ways, if ever, do we also say "I don't need you" in our church life with others? How does this attitude hurt the unity (interconnectedness) among members in the church?

3 Paul says that when each part of the church is working properly, "the church promotes the body's growth in building itself up in love." (Eph. 4:16) In the case of the girl in the diary, how was this achieved in her church?

Message

Church, in a biblical sense, transcends race, nationality, and culture. Yet, church in history, more often than not, consists of a particular ethnic group or race living in a particular social context with shared concerns and issues. For example, African American churches, Hispanic churches, Asian American churches minister mostly to their own racial/ethnic people. This, however, does not mean that they somehow have forgotten or ignored their calling for unity in Jesus Christ. We have to strive toward the unity as we all are already brothers and sisters in God. However, we also have to acknowledge that ethnic churches can carry out an important function for God's Kingdom—healing, nurturing and equipping the people for the Kingdom. In the case of the girl in the diary, she found God's caring love, healing, and affirmation from the members of her Korean American Christian youth group through prayer, Bible study, worship, and fellowship. She experienced the fullness of Jesus Christ through a Korean American church. Like her there are many other Korean Americans who experience healing of their emotional wounds, the sense of belonging as well as affirmation of their worth and value as God's children.

my spiritual home

Download & Apply

20 minutes

1 In what ways does your church and youth group function as the body of Christ? If you have experienced any healing, support, and encouragement through other members and the church leaders, please share with each other.

2 Each of us is an individual part of the church, the body of Christ. Name some ways you can become the body of Christ, contributing to the growth and well being of your church. How can you help your youth group or your church to be the body of Christ?

3 In what ways can we reach out to other Christians with different racial/ethnic backgrounds to promote and live out the unity of all Christians in Christ?

LESSON 8
Cracking the Code

News Feed

15 minutes

Tom is a Korean American who grew up in Fort Lee, a heavily Korean populated town in Northern New Jersey. His father and mother immigrated to America in the late 1970s, when he was three years old, and his brother was five. His father and mother ran a small grocery; he and his brother were raised mostly by their grandmother. In high school, Tom was not academically remarkable, barely above average in the class. After his high school, he went to the State University and majored in biology with a minor in math. Like many other Asian Americans, his parents thought the study of those subjects would get him a financially secure job either in a medical or a bio-engineering field. It was a safe and customary choice. However, his club activities at the college changed the course of his life. Tom discovered his true passion in arts, especially animated graphic design when he joined the school's Animation Club. In fact, drawing comic figures was his childhood passion, which he had forgotten for a long time. He had even earned several awards in local art contests. When his club displayed exhibitions during a school festival, Tom's works received the attention of a well-known computer graphic artist. With these encouragements Tom began to devote much of his time to graphic design and animation work. In his junior year, after long prayer and reflection he decided to switch his major into creative arts. His parents were not happy with his decision, worrying about his financial security in the future. They tried very hard to persuade him out of his renewed passion. Tom promised that he would do his best to be "a successful person," and not to disappoint them. He worked hard in his new passion. Tom further pursued his passion at a graduate school where he excelled beyond his own expectation. He was hired by Universal Studios after graduation, where he rose to the position of Creative Director. Tom now runs his own creative art/design studio in New Jersey with 12 employees.

Chat

1. What do you think of Tom's decision? What would you have done if you were Tom?

2. Why is it important to follow your passion?

3. Have you noticed that you are different from others in terms of your talents and gifts? Do you also notice different gifts among your brothers and sisters or friends? Are these differences a good or a bad thing?

Focus

Talents are qualities that you are naturally born with. These talents are gifts from God. For example, some are naturally fast runners, while others are naturally good singers. Every person is born with at least one or two special talents. Successful people are those who discover their talents early and nurture them with passion. However, the discovery of talents demands prayer (listening to one's heart) and careful observation of the self. Sometimes these talents are deeply hidden or confused with ambitions, other concerns and interests, thus making them difficult to identify. Other times our talents may not fit well with our own expectation and our parents' expectations (for example, in the above story, Tom's artistic talent was in conflict with his parents' desire for him to become an engineer or a doctor).

The Story of Seabiscuit

Seabiscuit was a legendary champion race horse in the U.S. Books were written and the movies were made about him. Yet, when he was a young colt, there was nothing noticeable; he was undersized, knobby-kneed, and lazy. He had a very unpromising start as a race horse. He was terribly hard to train. It was only after his unique bents were discovered by Tom Smith, his trainer, and used for the benefits of a race that he began to prosper. He was unlike other horses. Although he was a horse, he had unique talents. He fought any rider who pulled back on the reins to slow him down; he loved to stay close to the rail, and would run his fastest only there. So, if even a horse, such as Seabiscuit, is born with unique inclinations, how about human beings?

Text

20 minutes

Genesis 37:12-14

12 Now his [Joseph's] brothers had gone to graze their father's flocks near
Shechem, 13 and Israel said to Joseph, "As you know, your brothers are
grazing the flocks near Shechem. Come, I am going to send you to them."
"Very well," he replied. 14 So he said to him, "Go and see if all is well with your
brothers and with the flocks, and bring word back to me." Then he sent him
off from the Valley of Hebron. When Joseph arrived at Shechem,

Genesis 39:5-6; 22-23.

5 From the time he [Potiphar] put him [Joseph] in charge of his household
and of all that he owned, the LORD blessed the household of the Egyptian
because of Joseph. The blessing of the LORD was on everything Potiphar
had, both in the house and in the field. 6 So he left in Joseph's care everything he had; with Joseph in charge, he did not concern himself with anything except the food he ate. Now Joseph was well-built and handsome,

22 So the warden put Joseph in charge of all those held in the prison, and
he was made responsible for all that was done there. 23 The warden paid
no attention to anything under Joseph's care, because the LORD was with
Joseph and gave him success in whatever he did.

Scan

1 Please read the three stories regarding Joseph carefully. Among the three stories, what common features do you see in Joseph?

2 What talents can you identify in Joseph? What do you think he was good at?

3 How did God guide his life even under difficult conditions to nurture his talents?

Message

God created you as a unique/special person, and God knows who you are. Scripture says, "[Y]ou (God) created my inmost being; you knit me together in my mother's womb. I praise you because I am fearfully and wonderfully made" (Ps. 139: 13-14a). A very important part of knowing who we are involves discovering our God-given talents. If knowing who we are is important to living a happy and fulfilling life in God, discovering and nurturing our talents becomes an important step toward a happy life. (Revisit Ask Kevin) How then do we go about discovering our talents? One common way we discover our talents is by exploring and trying out different interests and activities in our life. Another way is to get the help of others, mentors and experts, to discover and confirm our talents.

Download & Apply

20 minutes

1 What talents do you think you have? How do your close friends, parents, teachers, siblings feel about what your talents are? Use the "IN SEARCH OF MY GIFTS" at the end of this chapter to answer this question.

2 Name some of the activities that you tried and explored recently that helped you to clarify your talents. What have you learned about yourself and your talents through these activities?

In Search of My Gifts

1 Observe what others say about you:

Listen to what those who are closest to you say about your talents and gifts. (i.e. Parents, teachers, pastors, counselors, siblings, friends and others) What do they say about you? Check off all the descriptions of talents/gifts that others have pointed out in you.

____ You are very athletic
____ You are funny and humorous
____ You are a good speaker/communicator
____ You are a good writer
____ You have a beautiful voice
____ You are a good singer
____ You are a good artist (painting, fine art, sculpture, design…etc)
____ You are so good with computers (Are you related to Bill Gates?)
____ You are a good dancer
____ You are a good leader
____ You are a good listener
____ You give good advice
____ You are very understanding
____ You have a good and kind heart
____ You are good in math/science
____ You are very intelligent (very sharp!)
____ You are good with your hands
____ You are very dependable
____ You are a good musician (instruments, composing, etc)
____ You are a good actor/actress
____ ________________________________
____ ________________________________
____ ________________________________

2 Make a self-observation

When you consider your past experiences of activities in school, church, retreat, camps, travel, volunteering and etc, name three talents and gifts you feel that you have.

I am good in (with) ______________________________

I am good in (with) ______________________________

I am good in (with) ______________________________

3 Learn about yourself

If you were to list three things that you really enjoy doing or feel passion ate about, what would they be (i.e. singing, caring for children, getting involved in the community... etc):

A ______________________________

B ______________________________

C ______________________________

4 Based on the above observation, what can you say about your God-given talents and gifts? (Note: Try to come back to this self-test every year and see how the answers change or remain the same through time)

LESSON 9

The Ten-Thousand-Hour Rule

News Feed

15 minutes

Jane is a first generation Korean American professor of criminology at a college in Chicago. She came to the U.S. to study criminology in her late twenties. She had a passion for the study of criminal behaviors as she loved to read mystery novels since her childhood. Her parents opposed her idea of studying overseas and pursuing the study of criminology. They said that such matters and subjects must be left to men. Her parents were also concerned about her safety away from home. They thought there were too many crimes in the U.S. Despite their opposition, she was determined to pursue her dream and came to the States. Yet, her life in the States was much tougher than she had expected.

Like many other first generation Korean Americans, Jane immediately experienced the challenge of language and cultural barriers. Several times she thought about giving up her study and going back to Korea, or going into a small business to make money. Yet her faith sustained her in her study. Through her church she received much moral and spiritual support that she needed to carry on. With the advice of others, she made several bold and smart decisions. Despite her financial challenges, she decided to subscribe to a local English newspapers and cable TV. She spent most of her free time watching cable news programs and reading newspapers. Sometimes she read the same news article several times to get used to contemporary English idioms and usages. These helped her not only to improve her English but also to obtain the updated knowledge of American society and culture. She also regularly read professional journals in her field in addition to her text books. Although her English was not fluent, she did not hesitate to make appointments with professors to ask questions and receive their advice. She routinely stayed up late into the night and wrote high quality term papers. During summers she interned at a local police station and correctional facilities to obtain field experience. Her passion and dedication to the study was increasingly acknowledged by her professors, and she was offered a research assistantship by a renowned professor. She assisted his projects and accompanied him to many different professional societies of criminology to further deepen her professional knowledge and to make connections with people in her field. While writing her dissertation, she presented papers at professional gatherings. Now she is a well-respected scholar in her field, having published several books and numerous articles and serves as an advisor for the police department of her city.

Chat

1 What is so remarkable about Jane?

2 What did Jane do to advance her talents? What challenges did she face and how did she overcome them?

3 How would you describe her attitude and approach to her goal? What can you learn from how she handled her challenges and seized her opportunities?

Focus

Behind the glory of successful people, there is a strong work ethic, intelligent use of time, and wise use of opportunities. Passion or talent alone does not lead us to success. Success in our profession is the result of passion and competence that comes from discipline and training. Talents are like jewels to be refined and processed. Without the discipline, they fade out or do not grow further; they cannot be used by others. Think about diamond ores; we cannot use them directly for rings, necklaces, etc. They have to be refined. Changrae Lee's (a famous Korean American fiction writer) advice for bourgeoning writers supports this truth:

"The only advice would be to read a lot and everything. And to have a lot of passion for it. Instead of wanting to be a writer, write. A lot of people want to be a writer, it seems to me, and they do everything they can to be a writer, except write." (from his interview with The Brown Daily Herald, March 10, 2008). The following biblical story tells a story that emphasizes the importance of making most of one's talents.

Did U Know?

"Why Can't I Do That!?"

Have you ever seen a professional golfer play golf or watched a golf tournament on TV and you wonder, "How on earth do they do what they do?!" Most of us often marvel at the amazing display of athletic skills by professional athletes, regardless of the sport they play. In case of golf, we marvel at the way Tour pros make the game look so easy, and ask, "Why can't I do that?" Well, the answer is quite simple: We don't practice as much as they do. The flipside of this simple answer is that all of us can become an expert in something, whether that something is sport, music, art, business, or whatever, if we just put our mind to it and practice consistently. Dr. Anders Ericsson, a renowned professor of psychology at Florida State University, argued that it takes approximately 10,000 hours of practice, which is about 10 years of time, to become an expert at any motor skill. Similar studies have shown that it takes 10 years before one can reach an elite level in any sport.

Back in 1973, Carnegie-Mellon researchers Drs. William Chase and Herbert Simon originally devised the 10-years-to-become-elite rule. Since then, numerous studies have supported their theory. In 1990s, veteran golf writers David Barrett and Al Barkow examined the careers of nine top PGA Tour pros and found that each had won their first major approximately 16 years after picking up a golf club for the first time. A lot of practice makes perfect! If you want to read more about this fascinating 10,000 hour theory about achieving greatness, read Malcom Gladwell's book *Outlier*, especially chapter 2.

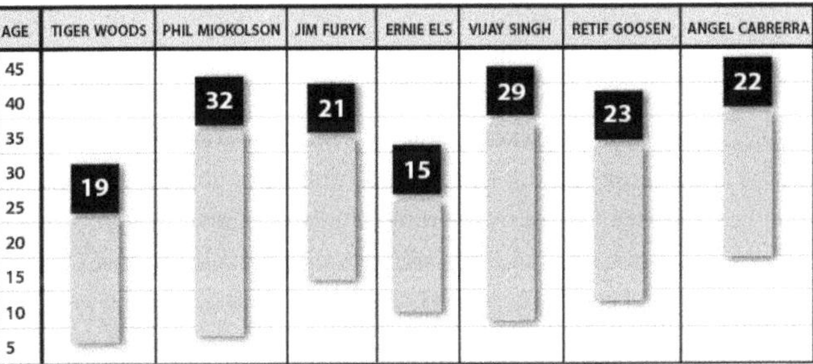

David DeNunzio, "The New Way to Improve," Gold Magazine, August 07, 2009. http://www.golf.com/golf/instruction/article/0,28136,1913844-5,00.html

Text

20 minutes

Matthew 25:14-30

14 "Again, it [the kingdom of heaven] will be like a man going on a journey,
who called his servants and entrusted his property to them. 15 To one he gave
five talents of money, to another two talents, and to another one talent, each
according to his ability. Then he went on his journey. 16 The man who had
received the five talents went at once and put his money to work and gained
five more. 17 So also, the one with the two talents gained two more. 18 But
the man who had received the one talent went off, dug a hole in the ground
and hid his master's money. 19 "After a long time the master of those servants
returned and settled accounts with them. 20 The man who had received the
five talents brought the other five. 'Master,' he said, 'you entrusted me with five
talents. See, I have gained five more.' 21 "His master replied, 'Well done, good
and faithful servant! You have been faithful with a few things; I will put you in
charge of many things. Come and share your master's happiness!' 22 "The man
with the two talents also came. 'Master,' he said, 'you entrusted me with two
talents; see, I have gained two more.' 23 "His master replied, 'Well done, good
and faithful servant! You have been faithful with a few things; I will put you in
charge of many things. Come and share your master's happiness!' 24 "Then the
man who had received the one talent came. 'Master,' he said, 'I knew that you
are a hard man, harvesting where you have not sown and gathering where
you have not scattered seed. 25 So I was afraid and went out and hid your
talent in the ground. See, here is what belongs to you.' 26 "His master replied,
'You wicked, lazy servant! So you knew that I harvest where I have not sown
and gather where I have not scattered seed? 27 Well then, you should have
put my money on deposit with the bankers, so that when I returned I would
have received it back with interest. 28 "'Take the talent from him and give it to
the one who has the ten talents. 29 For everyone who has will be given more,
and he will have an abundance. Whoever does not have, even what he has
will be taken from him. 30 And throw that worthless servant outside, into the
darkness, where there will be weeping and gnashing of teeth.'

Scan

1 Talk about the parable and its lessons. Where did the "talents" come from, and what is the servants' responsibility with them?

2 What was the mistake of the servant with one talent? Why was the servant so harshly rebuked by master?

3 Why is it important for Christians to "be faithful with a few things?" What did you learn from this parable?

Message

Nurturing talents is not easy. It requires discipline (focus and practice), which is often tedious, boring, and even a painful process. Talents, when not cultivated, may fade away. Therefore, sheer passivity (inactivity) is regarded as sin by Jesus in the parable. Nurturing talents is not necessarily individual personal work alone. It happens in a community through the support of friends, mentors and teachers. That is why life in a Christian community is so important.

Download & Apply

15 minutes

1 What do you think are your talents, and what kind of training and practices do you do to develop and nurture them? (e.g., extra curricular activities, taking lessons, internship, church activities, summer schools... etc.)

2 What prevents you from working hard to develop your talents? How can you improve the situation? Finally, do you have any mentors (at school, church, neighborhood, or home) who can help you to nurture your talents?

LESSON 10

Use It or Lose It!

News Feed

15 minutes

KJ Choi is a South Korean born world-renowned professional golfer. He grew up on a small island called Wan-do in the Southwest area of Korea that did not have a single golf course. And yet he has won many tournaments around the world, including 7 tournaments in the PGA tour. But KJ Choi is more than a world-class golfer. He is a devout Christian. On November 23rd, 2007, with 10 million dollars of seed money, Choi established a foundation in his name (The KJ Choi Foundation). The Foundation will offer philanthropic programs to assist adolescents from low-income families, cancer patients, and also offer scholarship programs for minority youths in the U.S. In the opening ribbon cutting ceremony of the Foundation, he said, "I am so delighted to establish the Foundation much earlier than I expected. Through the Foundation, I want to give hope for the youth living in challenging conditions and junior golf players." Even before the establishment of his foundation, Choi had been well known for his philanthropic actions; he donated $30, 000 for the victims of Hurricane Katrina. One of his ambitious future plans is to create the "KJ Junior Gold Team," which would consist of youngsters (5th-6th graders) with exceptional talents in golf. Choi wishes to teach them his golf skills and professional outlook in order to help them develop into world-class golfers. He wants to share his blessings with others through his mentoring and help youngsters to achieve their full potential and dreams in life.

Chat

1 What is most impressive to you about KJ Choi's story?

2 How do you see KJ Choi living out his Christian life and discipleship?

3 In what ways does he inspire people to serve and share their blessings with others?

Focus

God uses us for God's Kingdom. Talents are not only for our own benefit and success, but also for the common good of humanity, in particular, for the poor and the unfortunate people in our society. God grants us gifts and talents, and blesses us in order to benefit all God's children

Text

20 minutes

Who was Nehemiah?

Nehemiah was a second generation Jew exiled in Persia, who rose to the position of the cupbearer (a high ranking position, equivalent to a prime minister) to King Artaxerxes. At Nehemiah's time Judah was a province of the Persian Empire. Having heard distressing news about the destruction of the walls of Jerusalem, Nehemiah appealed to the King, and received a commission to be a governor of Judah to rebuild the walls. Despite various difficulties, he was able to not only rebuild the walls, but also initiated a series of legal, religious, and social reforms for the poor and marginal people of Judah. Nehemiah was a great biblical hero with strong compassion, love (1:4, "I sat down and wept. For some days I mourned and fasted and prayed before the God of heaven"), and perseverance (overcoming the oppositions of Sanballat, Tobiah, and Geshem) who not only voluntarily gave up his comfortable and luxurious life, but also used his talents of leadership (grasping the heart of the issues and encouraging and mobilizing people for a common cause), diplomacy (persuading King Artaxerxes to support his cause), communication and administration (with great organizational skills and managerial precision) for his people. By virtue of Nehemiah's sacrifice, the walls of Jerusalem were completed in about 52 days. Nehemiah is an inspiring example of a leader who used all of his gifts and energy for the glory of God.

Nehemiah 1:1-4

1 The words of Nehemiah son of Hacaliah: In the month of Kislev in the twentieth year, while I was in the citadel of Susa. 2 Hanani, one of my brothers, came from Judah with some other men, and I questioned them about the Jewish remnant that survived the exile, and also about Jerusalem. 3 They said to me, "Those who survived the exile and are back in the province are in great trouble and disgrace. The wall of Jerusalem is broken down, and its gates have been burned with fire." 4 When I heard these things, I sat down and wept. For some days I mourned and fasted and prayed before the God of heaven.

Nehemiah 2:1-9

1 In the month of Nisan in the twentieth year of King Artaxerxes, when wine was brought for him, I took the wine and gave it to the king. I had not been sad in his presence before; 2 so the king asked me, "Why does your face look so sad when you are not ill? This can be nothing but sadness of heart." I was very much afraid, 3 but I said to the king, "May the king live forever! Why should my face not look sad when the city where my fathers are buried lies in ruins, and its gates have been destroyed by fire?" 4 The king said to me, "What is it you want?" Then I prayed to the God of heaven, 5 and I answered the king, "If it pleases the king and if your servant has found favor in his sight, let him send me to the city in Judah where my fathers are buried so that I can rebuild it." 6 Then the king, with the queen sitting beside him, asked me, "How long will your journey take, and when will you get back?" It pleased the king to send me; so I set a time. 7 I also said to him, "If it pleases the king, may I have letters to the governors of Trans Euphrates, so that they will provide me safe-conduct until I arrive in Judah? 8 And may I have a letter to Asaph, keeper of the king's forest, so he will give me timber to make beams for the gates of the citadel by the temple and for the city wall and for the residence I will occupy?" And because the gracious hand of my God was upon me, the king granted my requests. 9 So I went to the governors of Trans-Euphrates and gave them the king's letters. The king had also sent army officers and cavalry with me.

Scan

1 Nehemiah was a cupbearer to the King (Nehemiah 1:11). What do you think is the significance of his position?

2 Why was Nehemiah so distressed in the story? How did he respond to the tragedy in Jerusalem?

3 Study his story further: How did he use his position and his gifts of diplomacy, administration, and leadership for his people?

4 What can you learn from Nehemiah? Why is it important to share our talents and blessings with others?

Message

God wants to use our talents and blessings that include social positions, achievements, wealth, and influences to build God's Kingdom and seek justice and peace for all. To be a disciple is to allow our talents and blessings to be used by God to meet the needs and sufferings of people in our community. As devoted disciples of Christ, we need to understand that giving and sharing of our talents and blessings should be more than just an occasional display of charity but a lifetime commitment.

Download & Apply

15 minutes

1 We don't need to be rich and famous in order to serve God and other people. Presume that you are a teacher, business person, social worker, store owner, etc.. How could you serve God and our Korean American community and society through your particular talents and blessings?

2 Where do you see the needs and sufferings in the Korean American community and our society? What would you do about them?

3 Why is it important to share our talents and blessings with others?

LESSON
Never Again

News Feed

15 minutes

The Los Angeles (LA) riots (April 29, 1992) was a very painful tragedy for many Korean Americans. The event was sparked by the acquittal of four white police officers accused in the videotaped beating of Rodney King, an African American man. When the news broke that the twelve-member jury with no African American member found the four white officers innocent of any crime, riots broke out in the South Central area of Los Angeles where Koreatown was located. The rioters primarily targeted Korean American stores. The riot damaged more than 1500 Korean stores, caused about 350 million dollars in damages, and resulted in the death of an 18-year-old Korean American college student, Edward Song Lee. It was heartbreaking to watch his mother crying over his blood-soaked body.

During the six-day riot, the LA police did not take any action to protect or defend Korean Americans and their property. The police just stood by, watching the rioters loot Korean-owned stores. The police did prevent the riots from moving up to Beverly Hills, a wealthy white area. The media depicted the riots primarily as an African American vs. Korean problem, blaming especially Korean American store owners' mistreatment of African American customers over the years. Even when Korean Americans complained to the police about the lack of protection during the riots, their voices were either ignored or not taken seriously by the police. Only after the riots subsided did Korean Americans realize that they were politically powerless, not having a voice in their larger community. As a result, many Korean American organizations including churches actively got involved in networking with other ethnic groups and empowered themselves by gaining a political and communal voice. Unfortunately some Korean American churches did not get involved in examining and reflecting upon the lessons that could have been learned from the LA riots.

Chat

1 What is your impression of this video? What stands out for you in this video of the LA Riots?

2 Why do you think the police deliberately stayed away from Koreatown while protecting the white, wealthier Beverly Hills area?

3 Why do you think the Korean community was politically powerless during the LA riots?

Focus

America is a multi-racial society but often the rights of minorities here get neglected. It is important for Korean Americans to realize that we need to engage in the wider communal and political decisions. As individuals we often find ourselves powerless to deal with many issues of racial injustice. And it is from this struggle that we have come to learn the importance of working together to deal with the problem of injustice. If we do not speak for ourselves, no one else will speak for us. The story of Nehemiah informs us of the importance of rebuilding our community through prayerfully working together.

Text

20 minutes

Nehemiah 2:17-19

17 Then I said to them, "You see the trouble we are in, how Jerusalem lies in ruins with its gates burned. Come, let us rebuild the wall of Jerusalem, so that we may no longer suffer disgrace." 18 I told them that the hand of my God had been gracious upon me, and also the words that the king had spoken to me. Then they said, "Let us start building!" So they committed themselves to the common good. 19 But when Sanballat the Horonite and Tobiah the Ammonite official, and Geshem the Arab heard of it, they mocked and ridiculed us, saying, "What is this that you are doing? Are you rebelling against the king?"

Nehemiah 2:17-19; 3:1-10

1 Then the high priest Eliashib set to work with his fellow priests and rebuilt the Sheep Gate. They consecrated it and set up its doors; they consecrated it as far as the Tower of the Hundred and as far as the Tower of Hananel. 2 And the men of Jericho built next to him. And next to them Zaccur son of Imri built. 3 The sons of Hassenaah built the Fish Gate; they laid its beams and set up its doors, its bolts, and its bars. 4 Next to them Meremoth son of Uriah son of Hakkoz made repairs. Next to them Meshullam son of Berechiah son of Meshezabel made repairs. Next to them Zadok son of Baana made repairs. 5 Next to them the Tekoites made repairs; but their nobles would not put their shoulders to the work of their Lord. 6 Joiada son of Paseah and Meshullam son of Besodeiah repaired the Old Gate; they laid its beams and set up its doors, its bolts, and its bars. 7 Next to them repairs were made by Melatiah the Gibeonite and Jadon the Meronothite-- the men of Gibeon and of Mizpah-- who were under the jurisdiction of the governor of the province Beyond the River. 8 Next to them Uzziel son of Harhaiah, one of the goldsmiths, made repairs. Next to him Hananiah, one of the perfumers, made repairs; and they restored Jerusalem as far as the Broad Wall.9 Next to them Rephaiah son of Hur, ruler of half the district of Jerusalem, made repairs. 10 Next to them Jedaiah son of Harumaph made repairs opposite his house; and next to him Hattush son of Hashabneiah made repairs.

Scan

1 Read Nehemiah 2:17. What disgrace is Nehemiah referring to?

2 Why was rebuilding the wall of Jerusalem important to Nehemiah and the Israelites? What does the wall symbolize for us?

3 The entire third chapter of the Book of Nehemiah is a list of all of the names and tasks of the individuals who participated in rebuilding the wall. Why do you think Nehemiah thought it important to make this exhaustive list? What can we learn from this story?

Message

The building of the wall symbolized repairing the well-being of the people as well as providing protection from invasions and dangers. This was a huge task that required the efforts and participation of a great number of people working together for the community. One of the lessons of the LA Riots was that the Korean American community did not have a "wall of well-being and protection" for times of crisis. Like Nehemiah, we need to come together and rebuild the symbolic wall of Korean American community. But at the same time we also need to engage in building up the larger community in which the Korean American community is a part. We need to build relationships with other minority communities, to build each other up. This is an important role for the church. Church is not only a place where we worship God on Sundays. Church is the people of God who are called to engage in God's work of justice and peace in society.

Download & Apply

15 minutes

1 How is your church or youth group currently involved in your community? Why is it important for Christians to be involved in the works for justice and equality for the Kingdom of God? (See Micah 6:8)

2 What are some of the ways we, as a youth group and church, can work together to "build the walls" of the Korean American community and thereby prevent such incidents like the LA Riots from happening again?

3 Working together is not always easy. What are some specific challenges and barriers that keep Korean Americans from working together effectively? What can we do to overcome these challenges?

LESSON

God's "GREEN" Beret

How Green Are You?

Do you think you are living a life of good stewardship by taking good care of the environment? Take a quick quiz below and see how informed and knowledgeable you are in environmental facts and care.

---

1 Approximately, how many species are disappearing from the earth every year?

a) 1000-5000
c) 10,000-20,000
b) 5000-10000
d) 20,000-100,000

---

2 What is the highest contributing factor to the green house effect?

a) motor vehicles
c) cows
b) deforestation
d) burning of coals

---

3 The Amazon Rainforest has been called as the "Lungs of the Earth" because it continuously recycles carbon dioxide into oxygen. What percentage of the world oxygen is produced in the Amazon Rainforest?

a) 7%
c) 20%
b) 15%
d) 30%

---

4 Polar bears are feeding on the ice catching seal pups and other sea animals. However, global warming increases sea temperature and consequently melts down glacier and the arctic ice where polar bears do hunting. About what percentage of polar bear population is likely to decline over next 30-50 years due to global warming?

a) 10%
c) 30%
b) 20%
d) 50%

---

5 What's the biggest consumer of power in homes?

a) Clothes dryer
c)Iron
b) Refrigerator
d) Hair dryer

6 The most common source of renewable energy in the world is:

a) solar
b) wind
c) geothermal
d) hydroelectric

---

7 The leading greenhouse gas is:

a) water vapor
b) methane
c) carbon dioxide
d) nitrous oxide

---

8 In 2005, renewable energy made up what percentage of total energy used in the U.S.?

a) 1%
b) 6%
c) 10%
d) 20%

---

9 The energy saved by recycling a can of Coke could run a TV for:

a) 15 minutes
b) half an hour
c) two hours
d) three hours

---

10 In the 2 minutes it takes for you to brush your teeth, how much water goes down the drain if you let the water run?

a) ½ gallon
b) 1 gallon
c) 2 gallons
d) 4 gallons

---

11 Every time you flush a standard toilet, you use ________ gallons of water.

a) 2.2 gallons
b) 4.5 gallons
c) 6.5 gallons
d) 9 gallons

---

12 A leaky faucet wastes up to ________ gallons of water a year?

a) 2700 gallons
b) 3200 gallons
c) 4500 gallons
d) 5000 gallons

---

13 Compact fluorescent lights (CFLs) use how much less energy than regular light bulbs

a) 45%
b) 55%
c) 65%
d) 75%

News Feed

15 minutes

Danny Seo is a second generation Korean American who has made a name for himself as an "environmental lifestyle expert." He is passionate about living an eco-friendly life and has become an expert communicator on the subject through his best-selling books, lectures, television programs, and magazine columns. He has been called the "eco-living consultant to the stars" and has become a leading authority on living an environmentally friendly lifestyle. Danny Seo was born on Earth Day in 1977 and when he was only 12 years old he founded "Earth 2000," an environmental group that became the largest environmental activist charity organization led by teenagers.

He is the author of several bestselling books on eco-friendly living as well as being the editor-at-large of Country Home magazine and writing a monthly column for its millions of readers. He is also the Environmental Lifestyle Contributor on The CBS Early Show, giving creative tips on how to live green with style.

Danny passionately communicates the importance of recycling and the importance of being good stewards of the environment. He has given hundreds of lectures at universities, corporations, and all kinds of special events. Danny Seo is inspiring younger and older generations to believe that to live an environmentally responsible life is a way to live life to the full. He is one Korean American who is making a difference by making the world greener.

Danny Seo
Eco-friendly stylist

Chat

1 What do you think about what Danny Seo is doing? Do you think what he is doing is important and special? If so why?

2 In light of the video clip that you just watched, why do you think that taking care of our environment is a serious duty of a Christian?

3 On a scale of one to ten, how would you rate your involvement in environmental issues? Test yourself by using the Assessment Questionnaire "How Green Are You?"

Focus

We are living in a critical time. Earth is suffering from overuse and exploitation. Global warming is threatening to destroy animals like the polar bear. As Christians we need to re-read the story of creation and understand thatit is our responsibility to take care of God's creation for the glory of God. We will look at the Genesis texts and do a word study on words like "dominion" and "cultivate."

Text

20 minutes

Genesis 1:26 & 28

26 "Then God said, "Let us make humankind in our image, according to our likeness; and let them have dominion over the fish of the sea, and over the birds of the air, and over the cattle, and over all the wild animals of the earth, and over every creeping thing that creeps upon the earth." 27 So God created humankind1 in his image, in the image of God he created them;2 male and female he created them. 28 God blessed them, and God said to them, "Be fruitful and multiply, and fill the earth and subdue it; and have dominion over the fish of the sea and over the birds of the air and over every living thing that moves upon the earth."

Genesis 2:15

"The LORD God took the man and put him in the garden of Eden to till it and keep it."

Psalm 147:7-9

7 Sing to the LORD with thanksgiving; make music to our God on the harp. 8
He covers the sky with clouds; he supplies the earth with rain and makes grass grow on the hills. 9 He provides food for the cattle and for the young ravens when they call.

God's "green" beret

The Hebrew word for Dominion (Gen. 1:26-18) is *radah* which means to "tread down," to "dominate," and to "subjugate." And this word was used mainly in the context of Hebrew Bible to describe the relationship between a king and his people. Having dominion, the king of Israel had covenantal responsibility to care for those whom he ruled. Therefore, dominion does not mean to exploit or to destroy but to exercise care and responsibility for God's domain particularly in the interest of those who are poor and marginalized.
(From "The Stewardship of Creation" by Russell A. Butkus, 2002, The Center for Christian Ethics at Baylor University.)

In Gen. 2:15 the "Lord took the man and put him in the garden of Eden to till it and keep it." The word for "till" in Hebrew is *abad* which means to serve it with reverence. The word for "keep" is *shamar* which means to guard, to watch, and to protect. Therefore, the command to till and keep the garden of Eden is a command to care for it with reverence and to protect it.

Scan

1 What images come to your mind when you think about the word "dominion"? How does the Hebrew understanding of "dominion" different from our popular notion of "domination"?

2 According to the passages in the box above, what are human responsibilities toward God's creation? What is Christian stewardship to you?

3 Read Genesis 1:22 ("God blessed them, saying, "Be fruitful and multiply and fill the waters in the seas, and let birds multiply on the earth") and Genesis 1:28. Genesis 1:22 is God's commandment to the animals and Genesis 1:28 is God's commandment to human beings. What do you think is God's desire for God's creation based upon these two verses?

4 What does the Psalm text (Psalm 147:7-9) say about who God is? What is God doing in this text? How does this text help us to understand our role in God's creation as "God's people"?

Christian Stewardship

A steward is a caretaker. She or he is someone who manages another's property, finances, or someone who is in charge of the household affairs of a large estate, club, hotel, or resort. Christian stewardship is the notion that we are God's stewards. All things we have and use—our body, our health, our possessions, our intellect, our talents, and natural resources—are given by God; therefore we can neither claim their ownership nor be allowed to misuse them. They belong to God because God created all things (Creation is God's large estate and we are caretakers!). As the parable of the Talents (Matthew 25:14-30) teaches us, we will be held accountable to God for what we do with these gifts and resources that God has entrusted to us.

Message

To be a Christian means more than just believing in Jesus as our personal Lord and Savior. It means that we live as good stewards or managers of God's creation. This includes caring about our environment and being responsible for what God has given us. We are created by God to live with and take care of the rest of God's creation and not merely use and exploit it. It is important to remember that taking care of our environment and God's creation is just one aspect of being good stewards of God.

Citizens of the Kingdom

In addition to the stewardship of creation, it is also important for us as Korean American Christians to see ourselves as citizens of God's Kingdom who are called to work for peace, justice, and well-being (shalom) of the world. This means that we are also called to work toward relieving poverty, violence, preventing genocides, wars and all kinds of abuses around the world. The churches must come together to work for the Kingdom of God and the well-being of all of God's creation.

Download & Apply

15 minutes

1 What are ways that our society abuses God's creation?

2 What can you do to be better stewards of God's creation? Can you think of some things you can do immediately to have a positive effect on the environment? Break into groups of 3-5 people and brainstorm few short-term (4- week-long) projects that can be done in your church or homes. Choose one project that your group will undertake, then share it with the rest of the group.

3 In addition to getting involved with ecological issues, what are some other ways that your youth group can get involved to make a positive impact in our society and the world? (For example, cleaning up the neighborhood, feeding the poor and the homeless, seeking reconciliation with other ethnic/ racial groups, conserving energy, initiating recycling in your church, starting a composting project in your church, etc.)

About Authors

Hak Joon Lee is the Associate Professor of Theology and Ethics at New Brunswick Theological Seminary. Lee received his Ph.D. degree from Princeton Theological Seminary, and has published several books, including *Covenant and Communication: A Christian Moral Conversation with Jürgen Habermas, We Will Get to the Promised Land: Martin Luther King, Jr.'s Communal-Political Spirituality, Bridge Builders*, and numerous articles. He was a keynote speaker for the celebration of Martin Luther King, Jr.'s birthday in several cities of NJ and NY. An ordained minister of Word and Sacrament in the PC (USA), he has been engaging interracial and intercultural issues for over 20 years, and recently founded G2G Christian Education Center, a research institute on Asian American Christianity and Culture, for the empowerment of Asian American churches.

Kevin Park is an Associate for Theology in the Office of Theology and Worship in the Presbyterian Church (USA) headquarters in Louisville, Kentucky, focusing on theological and ministry issues arising from racial ethnic churches. He is an ordained Presbyterian pastor and has 20 years of experience doing ministry with youth and college students as well as with American and Korean adults. He worked as an Assistant Director of Asian American Program at Princeton Theological Seminary as well as an adjunct professor of theology at New Brunswick Seminary. He earned his Ph.D. in Systematic Theology from Princeton Theological Seminary in 2002, writing his dissertation on emerging Korean American theologies and the theology of the cross.

Kil Jae Park is the senior pastor of Teaneck United Methodist Church in Teaneck, NJ and an adjunct professor of Christian education at New Brunswick Theological Seminary. With his Ph.D. in Christian Education from Princeton Theological Seminary, he has been contributing articles to journals and magazines for more than 10 years on the issues of Korean American identity, family ministry and Christian education. With more than 20 years of ministry working with children, youth, and college students, he is a highly sought speaker in Korean American churches nationwide, giving many workshops and seminars for pastors, teachers, and parents.

www.ingramcontent.com/pod-product-compliance
Ingram Content Group UK Ltd.
Pitfield, Milton Keynes, MK11 3LW, UK
UKHW020240250726
13967UKWH00001B/480